The Fall

Lisa F

BookLeaf
Publishing

Presentation by *BookLeaf Publishing*

Web: www.bookleafpub.com

E-mail: info@bookleafpub.com

ISBN: 9789395950831

First edition 2022

*Thank you to my daughter for showing me
the only true love that exists.*

PREFACE

You know I'm bad at love - Halsey

Chernobyl

I have no poem for you this time
No feelings left, you uninspire me
Like the site of a nuclear meltdown
You, a mere human, couldn't survive
Yet strangely, in your absence
the undergrowth is lush
And the fruit abundant.

Arashi

The wind pounds against the window
I'm sleepless and tense
The forecast echos
Danger beware stay safe
Despite warnings
Of the inevitable
The urge to enter the storm
Is nearly unbearable.
Forehead pressed against the cool glass
I close my eyes and imagine,
Smiling,
of giving in to temptation.

A fairytale. Ending.

I had lost the ability to feel
When you woke me up
Blood rushing, heart pounding
Occupying all my thoughts

You said you felt the same
imagined what it would be like
to risk believing
in the one.

But we're jaded. And you broke first.
Better the devil.
You know true love is a lie.
All love ends in tragedy.

"What about happily ever after?"
In the silence your answer echoed
"It's a fairytale. Everyone
settles in the end."

I miss -it-

Juxtaposed against my
longing is your silence

. . . .

. . . .

. . . .

So, I throw my
emotions
at it

. . . .

. . . . . .

. . . . .

Then, like laughing in space,
the vacuum of your
silence eats up
my words

. . . .

. . .

. .

And the volume of your
response is louder
than mine. As if
-it- didn't exist
at all

.

Drowning

I cling to you,
Though I know drowning is inevitable.
Clutching at the straws of you.
Piled high; memories of you.
And me. Happy. Because we were.
Sometimes.
And those memories of happiness,
Are my straws.
Yet this ocean of your discontent is slowly
filling my lungs.
But love, I'd rather death than life.
Without you.

Leaving

You are moving
I am fixed
Here in bed
Immobile
Knowing that
The distance between us
When we fell in love
Is also the distance between us
Now
As you leave.
The circle completes itself
Missing by miles.

Here we are Floating in Space

I remember once.
Once when I felt the loss of love with so much
force
it shattered my soul.
The absence of my beloved
a black hole
in the universe of my body,
pulling everything my life contained
into the gaping maw
of longing,
Longing for the bright star that once was.

I remember the feeling.
Horrible and beautiful all at the same time.
Sometimes,
 I wish I could feel like that again.
Love as a solar entity,
whose gravitational pull could keep me
fixed in orbit.

It's different now.
I'm just a rock floating in space.
Feeling the pull of gravitation
yet managing to fly on my course

only slightly altered,
no longer wishing to become a satellite to
someone else's path.
But with loss of guidance sometimes I feel lost.
Without purpose.
Just a floating rock
unable to support
even a trace of life.

Maybe one day,
I will have oceans,
mountains,
forests and sky.
So here I am floating in space,
left with the question,
"How do I attract to me the necessary
ingredients for life?"
"How do I make this barren rock abundant?"

What do I like about you?

What do I like about you?
What makes you different?
I ponder the answer eating toast.
And whilst you have many appealing parts.
Others have these as well. They aren't
uncommon.
And whilst you are kind and caring,
These too are qualities held by more than a few.
So what do I like about you?
I suppose it's this.
Your opinions.
Not just any opinions but ones based in fact.
Fact, experience and research.
A rare find
such opinions
attached to a cock that is useful.

Fear

Is the fear of being alone
really worse that this
boredom?

The Price of Love

She'd gotten used to being a slut,
Somehow it felt empowering to be the master of
her sexuality.
Feminism said she was strong. Men said she was
powerful.
But now she'd put a price on it and somehow
that made it different.
Feminism says she is a victim.
Men say she is not to be trusted.
Even her heart gets caught up in the stigma and
tells her she is unworthy of being loved.
I guess it's true what they say.
Money changes everything.

Fever Dream

Hot, thrashing,
naked body exposed
Slender leg seeking
The coolness of night air
Unkempt hair
Unshaven
Unruly
Desire but a memory
Hot flushes are now
Only Hormonal.

Kissing

Remember when a kiss could make the rest of
the world disappear?
Have the kisses gotten worse
Or has the world just gotten too big
to ignore?

Knowledge is Power

The knowledge that true love
Is fantasy
Feels disempowering.
It seems,
so much of life is based
On that construct of true love.
Oh well.
Maybe I just need an emotional support animal?

That's How You Make a Life

Good job
Steady income
Mortage in a nice suburb.
Reliable partner
Some animals
Some kids
A family car
Arguments over affection
Arguments over housework
Arguments over money
Arguments over why you just can't do that one
thing I asked!
Silence rather than arguments

Why don't we talk anymore?

Time

It seemed like it would last forever.
Youth.
Us.
That feeling.
But the cracks that started slowly
Progressed quickly.
And in time
Even the heaped ruins
became as
faded as the old photographs

Ember

Through it all
A small spark still waits
After all this time.
Would seeing you again
Reignite its flame?
Or finally put it to rest?

Close my eyes

25 years on
And
if I close my eyes I can still
remember the power of your lips
On mine
And how after they were I couldn't even
remember where I was.
Remembering how forgetting
Was such fun.

Myself

Sitting here alone
At least I can't disappoint anyone else.

www.ingramcontent.com/pod-product-compliance
Lightning Source LLC
LaVergne TN
LVHW010024200726

843495LV00015B/1917